CHRISTMAS
HEIRLOOM PATTERNS
FOR WOODCARVING

VOLUME II

ROSS OAR

ELEVEN DETAILED PATTERNS WITH FULL COLOR PICTURES AND, STEP BY STEP PHOTOGRAPHS TO CARVE A SANTA ORNAMENT.

ACKNOWLEDGEMENTS
To my Children, Eric, Jennifer and Ross, Jr.
who's artistic talents will continue into the next generation.

PUBLISHED BY
West Falls Woodcarving 7458 Ellicott Road, West Falls, NY 14170

PRINTED BY
Swyers Printing / Four Centre Drive, Quaker Centre
Orchard Park, NY 14127

PHOTOGRAPHS AND BOOK DESIGN LAYOUT BY
Pencil In The River Studio, Inc. / 5460 Transit Road, Depew, NY 14043

Member of the National Wood Carvers Association,
7424 Miami Avenue, Cincinnati, OH 45243. Southtowns Woodcarvers of Western New York,
Niagara Frontier Woodcarvers, Calusa Wood Carvers.

CONTENTS

❖ ❖ ❖

HELPFUL CARVING HINTS

❖ ❖ ❖

START YOUR CARVING BY TRACING THE PATTERN ON YOUR BASSWOOD BLOCK OR WOOD OF PREFERENCE, USING BOTH THE SIDE AND THE FRONT VIEW. MAKE SURE THE HEAD IS GOING WITH THE GRAIN OF THE WOOD IN THE VERTICAL POSITION. IF YOU HAVE A BANDSAW, CUT OUT YOUR BLANK OR USE A POWER OR HAND SAW THAT WILL ENABLE YOU TO MAKE YOUR CUTOUT. AFTER YOU HAVE YOUR CUTOUT, START TO ROUND OFF THE EDGES OF THE WOOD WITH YOUR BENCH KNIFE AND LARGE GOUGES. DRAW ON THE WOOD IN PENCIL BEFORE YOU CARVE A SPECIFIC AREA. TAKE YOUR TIME, "KEEP YOUR TOOLS SHARP," CHECK FREQUENTLY THE COLORED PICTURE AND PATTERN TO MAKE SURE YOU ARE TAKING OFF THE CORRECT AREAS OF WOOD.

USE THE PACK SANTA ORNAMENT STEP-BY-STEP FOR GUIDANCE.

WOODCARVING IS A VERY REWARDING HOBBY THAT YOU WILL FIND VERY RELAXING. WITH PRACTICE YOU WILL LEARN TO DO DIFFERENT PROJECTS AND CONTINUE TO IMPROVE YOUR CARVING SKILLS. **"HAVE FUN!"**

TOOLS USED FOR CARVINGS IN THIS BOOK

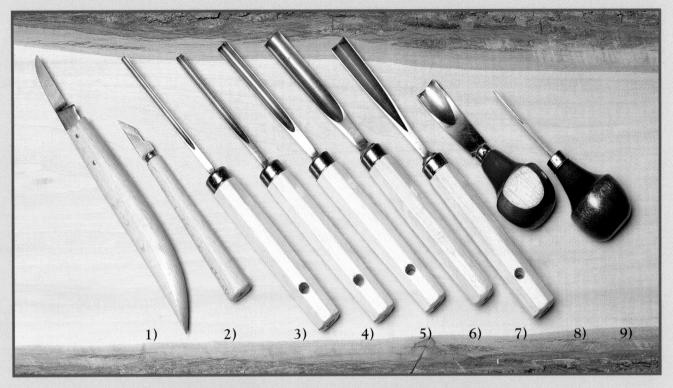

1) BENCH KNIFE
2) SMALL FINE POINTED
   TYPE KNIFE
3) 2MM #10 GOUGE
4) 4MM #10 GOUGE
5) 6MM #10 GOUGE

6) 12MM #10 GOUGE
7) 10MM 75° "V" GOUGE
8) 5/8" BENT PALM
   #9 GOUGE
9) 1/16" STRAIGHT PALM
   #9 GOUGE

MISCELLANEOUS MATERIALS: TRACING PAPER, MEDIUM & FINE SHARPENING STONE, LEATHER STROP, PAINT AND BRUSHES. WE USED ARTISTS OILS FOR THE PICTURED CARVINGS. "KEEP TOOLS SHARP AT ALL TIMES, A SHARP TOOL MAKES A SHARP CARVING."

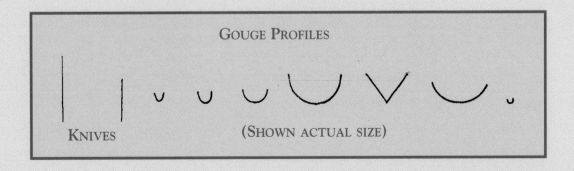

GOUGE PROFILES

KNIVES   (SHOWN ACTUAL SIZE)

PACK SANTA ORNAMENT

COMPLETED SIDE (#25) VIEW OF VERSION ONE
WITH FOLDED ARMS

FINISHED FRONT (#26) VIEW VERSION ONE

THE OTHER IS A SKY DIVING PACK SANTA ORNAMENT. FOLLOW THE DOTTED LINES AND GLUE ON THE ARMS SEPARATE. STEP-BY-STEP CHANGES FOR VERSION 2 "SKYDIVING PACK SANTA" ON PAGE 32.

THIS PACK SANTA ORNAMENT CAN BE MADE TWO WAYS. ONE WITH ARMS FOLDED IN. (AS SHOWN IN COLOR PHOTOGRAPH)

ACTUAL SIZE OF ORIGINAL 5 1/2" HEIGHT

(1)
BAND SAWED BLANK WITH
PENCILED PATTERN

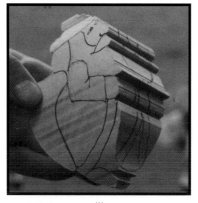

(2)
PENCILED SIDE & FRONT VIEW

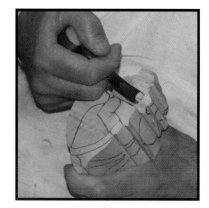

(3)
USING A 5/8" BENT PALM #9 GOUGE
& KNIFE-ROUGH OUT THE HEAD

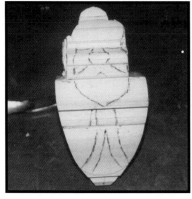

(4)
FRONT VIEW OF HEAD ROUGHED
OUT- SHOWING PENCIL DRAWING

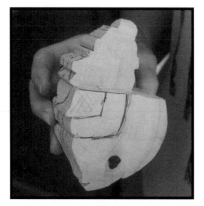

(5)
SIDE VIEW OF HEAD
AFTER BEING ROUGHED OUT

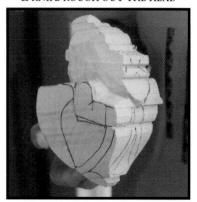

(6)
QUARTER VIEW AFTER ROUGHING
OUT HEAD, ARM AND BEARD

(7)
ROUGHING OUT OF COAT

(8)
ROUGHED OUT COAT

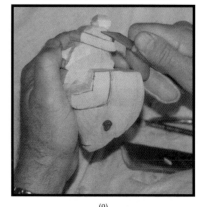

(9)
WORKING ON HAT-
ROUNDING CORNERS

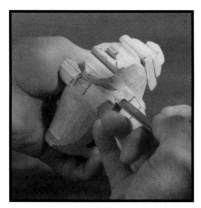

(10)
USING "V" GOUGE CUT ELBOW LINE-
NOTE "V" GOUGE ALSO USED TO
MAKE FOLDS IN COAT AT JOINTS

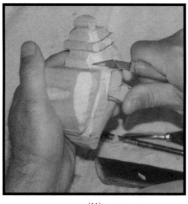

(11)
TAKE TIME TO SHARPEN OR STROP
TOOLS FOR DISTINCT CUT
(FORMING HAIR)

(12)
OUTLINING PACK WITH
"V" TOOL

(13)
FINISHING THE ROUGH OUT
OF COAT

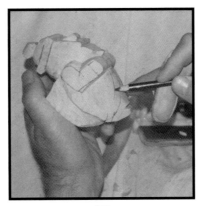

(14)
REMARK COAT LINE

(15)
FACE DETAILS STARTED-
NOSE & MUSTACHE FORMED

(16)
STOP CUTS FOR MAKING
EDGE ON THE HAT

(17)
ROUNDING OFF THE PACK

(18)
DRAW EAR ON & OUTLINE
WITH "V" TOOL

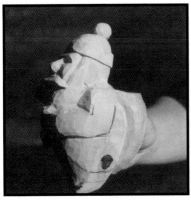

(19)
ROUGHED OUT LEFT SIDE VIEW

(20)
ROUGHED OUT RIGHT SIDE VIEW

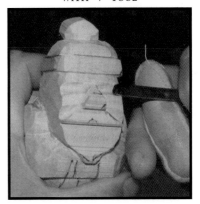

(21)
CREATING EYE SOCKETS WITH A
6MM #10 GOUGE

(22)
ROUGHING OUT FACIAL FEATURES
USING KNIFE

(23)
QUARTER VIEW
READY FOR DETAIL

(24)
PENCIL MARK FOR
HOLE IN PACK

7

MINIATURE FATHER CHRISTMAS

CARVE A HOLE IN PACK TO GLUE GIFTS
OR KEEP CLOSED, AS SHOWN

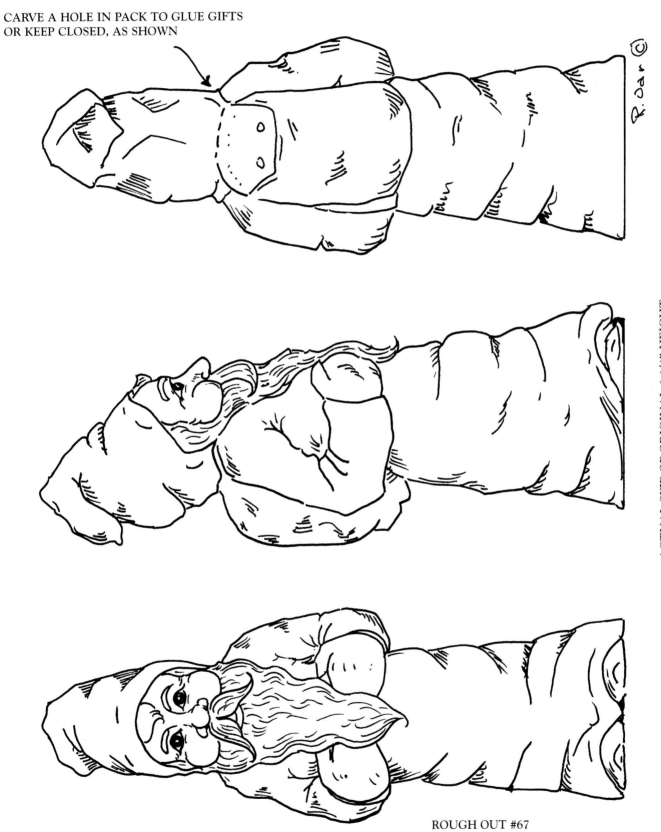

R. Jar ©

ACTUAL SIZE OF ORIGINAL 6 1/4" HEIGHT

ROUGH OUT #67

MRS. SANTA CLAUS

BY PUSHING A POINTED KNIFE
AROUND THE NECK LINE AT THE
ANGLE OF THE DASHED LINES,
THE HEAD CAN BE SLIGHTLY
TWISTED FOR DIFFERENT HEAD
POSITIONS.

BASKET OF
APPLES OR
SANTAS LUNCH

R. Dav ©

ACTUAL SIZE OF ORIGNAL 7 3/4" HEIGHT

11

SANTA IN ROCKER
CHECKING LIST

EYE GLASSES AND CHECK -LIST ARE MADE
OF PAPER CLIPS AND TIN CAN MATERIAL

NOTE:
SEE EYE GLASSES
ON PAGE 17

R. Oar ©

LEGS AND ROCKERS ARE
MADE OF WELDING ROD
SOLDERED TOGETHER AND
STUCK INTO BOTTOM OF
SEAT, OR CAN BE MADE OF
WOOD AND GLUED IN SEAT

ACTUAL SIZE OF ORIGINAL 7 3/4" HEIGHT

R. Oar ©

ROLLY POLLY SANTA HEAD

CUT OR DRILL HOLE AT
DASHED LINES AND FILL WITH
LEAD OR OTHER WEIGHTS

ROUGH OUT #63

ACTUAL SIZE OF ORIGINAL
7 1/4" HEIGHT

R. Oar ©

15

SANTA CLAUS

USING A PAPER CLIP AND BENDING AS SHOWN HERE, EYE GLASSES CAN BE ADDED

CARVE A DOLL OR OTHER ITEM AND INSERT HERE

R. Oar ©

ROUGH OUT #39

ACTUAL SIZE OF ORIGINAL 10 1/2" HEIGHT

R. Oar ©

17

SANTA'S ELVES

STOOL IS MADE
SEPARATE

CANE, HAMMER OR
OTHER OBJECTS
CAN BE PUT IN HIS
HAND

NOTE: THIS ELF
CAN ALSO BE MADE
TO RIDE SANTA'S
REINDEER FROM
VOLUME #1,
CHRISTMAS
HEIRLOOM
PATTERNS FOR
WOODCARVING

R. Oar ©

ACTUAL SIZE OF ORIGINAL 7"

SANTA ON LUGE

R. Oar ©

DRAWING IS ACTUAL SIZE WITH LUGE

SANTA ON LUGE
TOP IS ONE PIECE OF WOOD,
RUNNERS ARE MADE OF
COAT HANGERS OR CARVED
FROM SEPARATE WOOD.

WHEN YOU BAND SAW THE
BLANK USE ONLY TWO
VIEWS THE SIDE AND TOP

21

SANTA ON LUGE

NOTE:
THIS PATTERN WILL REQUIRE MORE
CARVING AFTER BAND SAWING, BECAUSE
THE BASE AND FIGURE ARE ONE PIECE
OF WOOD

DRAWING IS ACTUAL SIZE OF ORIGINAL WITH LUGE

SANTA ON LUGE

DRAWING IS ACTUAL SIZE OF ORIGINAL WITH LUGE

WAVING SANTA

CARVING CAN BE DONE
WITH OR WITHOUT
TOY SACK

ROUGH OUT #64

ACTUAL SIZE OF ORIGINAL WITHOUT
BASE 5 1/2" HEIGHT

R. Oar ©

25

HANGING SPIRAL SANTA
ORNAMENT

ROUGH OUT #73

R. Oar ©

ACTUAL SIZE OF ORIGINAL 8 1/4" HEIGHT

TOY SOLDIER

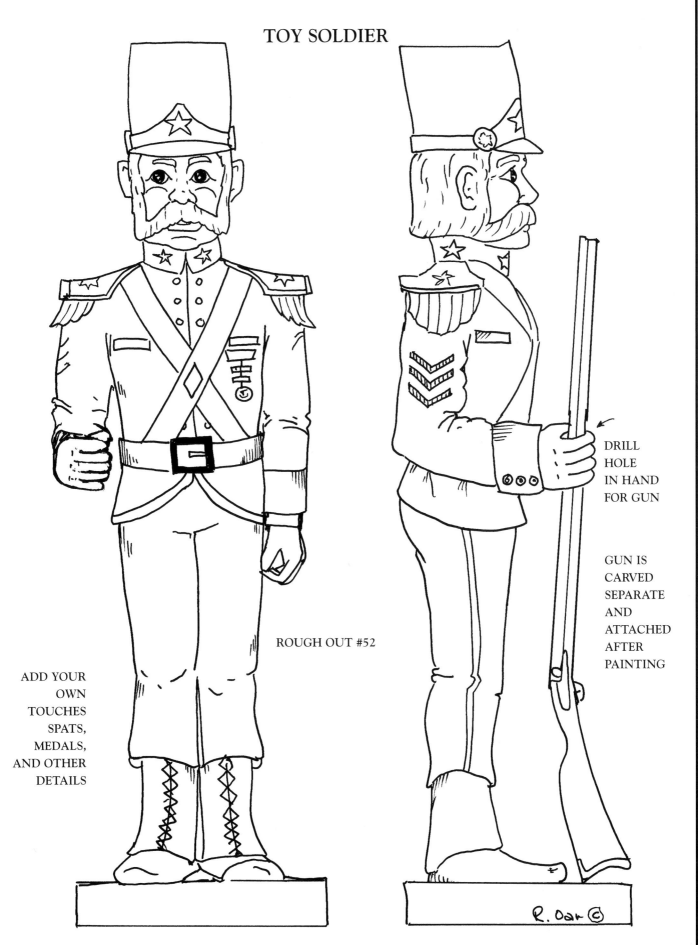

ROUGH OUT #52

ADD YOUR
OWN
TOUCHES
SPATS,
MEDALS,
AND OTHER
DETAILS

DRILL
HOLE
IN HAND
FOR GUN

GUN IS
CARVED
SEPARATE
AND
ATTACHED
AFTER
PAINTING

R. Oar ©

ACTUAL SIZE OF ORIGINAL 13" HEIGHT

DESIGN AND PAINTING TECHNIQUES

Many times when I create a Santa it is based on my observations or experiences of something happening at a special time. One example is the "Santa on Luge" which was inspired while watching the last Winter Olympic event.

When starting to design a new Santa, I do several thumbnail sketches of different poses. Then make the final drawing of the full profile and face views. This is transferred to the appropriate size of wood with the grain in the proper direction, usually the length of the piece. Quite often I will also model in clay allowing more freedom for action and movement, etc. This I will use as a model to carve from. When the carving is completed, paint using tube oils thinned with linseed oil and turpentine. In using oils drying time is your biggest problem. Cobalt Siccative drier improves this time. Drier is used with all oil colors using manufacturing directions. Starting with the face, mix flesh with a slight amount of yellow and burnt umber to produce the ruddy complexion. Before dry, stipple small amounts of red on the high spots. Example; cheeks, nose, ears, chin, forehead, etc. For eyes use a very fine brush #000 for painting white on the complete eye ball. With a deep blue or burnt umber put in the pupil after the white is dry. When pupil is totally dry create a highlight with a speck of white.

Then go on to the other white areas, again using the drier to speed the drying process. When all white is completely dry start your red paint, with drier added. I usually cut in with a #000 and then fill balance in with a #2 or #5 paint brush. While the red is still wet, shadow in low spots (wrinkles, under arm, etc.) with a darker red and stipple.

When the carving is completely dry, coat surface with a satin clear polyurethane. (Make sure it is completely dry before coating or the polyurethane will smear the paint.) When polyurethane is completely dry, 24 hours or more use a light wash of burnt umber, linseed oil and turpentine coat over the carving-immediately wiping entire carving with a soft cloth (old tee shirt) to create an antique affect.

VOLUME I

VOLUME II

For a brochure of rough out basswood blanks send SASE to:

West Falls Woodcarving, 7458 Ellicott Road, West Falls, N.Y. 14170

BASSWOOD ROUGH OUTS AVAILABLE FROM VOLUME I & VOLUME II

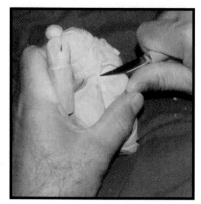

(A)
VIEW OF FLAT SHOULDER

(B)
CUT OFF ARMS & FLATTEN
SHOULDER TO APPLY EXTENDED ARM

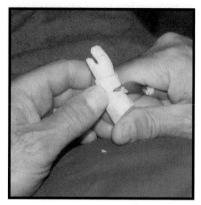

(C)
CARVE ARM BY USING KNIFE

(D)
CARVED ARM
READY FOR GLUING

VERSION TWO
"SKYDIVING
PACK SANTA"

STEP-BY-STEP
PICTORIAL
INSTRUCTIONS
"A-J"

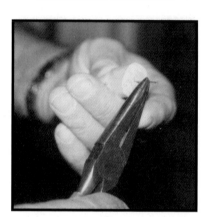

(E)
ADD PIN MADE FROM SMALL NAIL
FOR SUPPORT

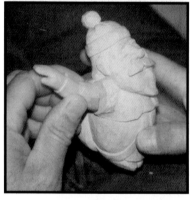

(F)
GLUE FINISHED ARMS IN POSITION

(G)
BACK VIEW SHOWING ARMS GLUED

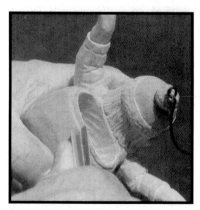

(H)
FINISHED TOP VIEW OF BACK PACK

(I)
FINISHED SIDE VIEW OF FACE

(J)
FINISHED CARVING WITH DETAILS